THE POWER OF MONEY:

Unleashing The Potential Within

BY

GEORGE L. STUBBS

Copyright © George L. Stubbs 2024. All rights reserved.

Before this document is duplicated or reproduced in any manner, the publisher's consent must be gained. Therefore, the contents within can neither be stored electronically, transferred, nor kept in a database. Neither in Part nor full can the document be copied, scanned, faxed, or retained without approval from the publisher or creator.

TABLE OF CONTENTS

CHAPTER 1 4

THE PSYCHOLOGY OF MONEY 4

CHAPTER 2 8

MONEY AND HAPPINESS 8

CHAPTER 3 13

MONEY AND RELATIONSHIPS 13

CHAPTER 4 17

MONEY AND PERSONAL GROWTH 17

CHAPTER 5 21

MONEY AND SOCIETY 21

CHAPTER 6 26

MONEY AND SPIRITUALITY 26

CONCLUSION 31

CHAPTER 1

THE PSYCHOLOGY OF MONEY

Money maintains a unique influence over our lives, not just in its actual form but also in the psychological space it occupies. Our relationship with money is profoundly established in our ideas, values, and experiences, determining our actions and attitudes toward prosperity, success, and abundance.

Money as a Symbol of Value and Worth:

From a young age, we are taught to link money with value and worth. It becomes a measure of our success, ability, and even our self-worth. The more money we have, the more successful and valuable we feel ourselves to be. This link between money and value frequently leads to a continuous chase of wealth, driven by a need for affirmation and prestige.

The Impact of Childhood Experiences on Money Mindset:

Our ideas and behaviors surrounding money are significantly shaped by our upbringing and early experiences. Messages received from parents, caregivers, and society at large impact our attitudes regarding money, success, and plenty. For some, growing up in an atmosphere of scarcity instills a fear-based worldview, marked by hoarding and anxiety about money. Others may have been raised with an abundant attitude, where money is considered a tool for growth and opportunity.

The Psychology of Spending and Saving Habits:

Our spending and saving habits are frequently a reflection of our underlying ideas and emotions surrounding money. Impulse buying, excessive consumption, or obsessive saving can all be expressions of underlying psychological wants or concerns. Understanding the psychological reasons underlying our financial actions is vital for gaining control over our finances and making deliberate decisions aligned with our objectives and beliefs.

Overcoming Limiting Beliefs about Money:

Many of us hold limiting views about money that keep us bound in patterns of scarcity and lack. Beliefs such as "money is scarce," "I don't deserve wealth," or "rich people are greedy" can impede our financial success and prevent us from attaining our full potential. By identifying and questioning these assumptions, we may begin to transform our thinking towards plenty and abundance.

Cultivating a Mindset of Abundance:

An abundance mindset is built on the conviction that there is more than enough to go around — enough riches, opportunity, and resources for everyone to prosper. Cultivating this attitude requires concentrating on plenty rather than scarcity, practicing thankfulness for what we have, and embracing a feeling of possibility and potential. With an abundant attitude, we may attract more riches and prosperity into our lives while simultaneously enjoying more pleasure and fulfillment.

In summation, our connection with money is complicated and multidimensional, impacted by a plethora of psychological aspects. By understanding the psychology of money, we can begin to untangle the attitudes and habits that hold us back and build a mentality of wealth and success. Through self-awareness, reflection, and deliberate action, we may harness the power of money to build a life of wealth, fulfillment, and meaning.

CHAPTER 2
MONEY AND HAPPINESS

Money and happiness have a complicated relationship that extends beyond basic cause and effect. While money may give comfort and security, its capacity to create permanent happiness is often misinterpreted. In this chapter, we will examine the complexity of this connection, evaluating the role of money in our search for pleasure and identifying ways to obtain real contentment.

The Relationship Between Money and Happiness:

At first look, it may appear natural to conclude that more money leads to more pleasure. After all, money may provide us the chance to acquire material belongings, travel to exotic countries, and indulge in life's joys. However, multiple studies have demonstrated that the association between money and happiness is more subtle than we may imagine.

Research undertaken by psychologists and economists has repeatedly revealed that while money can improve pleasure up to a certain extent, its influence reduces once fundamental requirements are addressed. This phenomenon is commonly referred to as the "hedonic treadmill," when individuals adjust to gains in income and find themselves no happier than they were before.

Beyond Materialism:

One of the important conclusions from the study of money and pleasure is the awareness that material goods give only transitory satisfaction. The excitement received from buying a new automobile or the latest technology is typically short-lived, giving rise to a yearning for the next major purchase. This cycle of consuming can lead to a never-ending drive for more, maintaining a sense of dissatisfaction and restlessness.

In contrast, research has shown that experiences offer greater enjoyment than material assets. Whether it's going to a new nation, attending a concert, or spending time with loved ones, experiences have a lasting influence on our well-being. Unlike material items, which lose their novelty with time, experiences give memories that may be cherished for a lifetime, adding to a sense of fulfillment and contentment.

Redefining Success and Satisfaction:

In a society that connects success with riches and position, it may be tough to rethink our concepts of success and contentment. However, genuine pleasure rests not in the amassing of riches but in living a life aligned with our beliefs and passions.

Rethinking our notion of success entails moving our attention from external indicators of performance to interior measurements of fulfillment. Instead of evaluating success by the size of our money accounts or the prestige of our occupations, we might evaluate elements like as our feeling of purpose, the quality of our relationships, and our general well-being.

Practices for Cultivating Gratitude and Contentment:

Cultivating thankfulness is one of the most potent methods to boost our feeling of pleasure and well-being. By concentrating on what we have rather than what we lack, we may build an attitude of abundance and gratitude for the benefits of our lives. Simple actions such as maintaining a gratitude notebook, expressing thanks to others, and experiencing life's minor joys may dramatically improve our overall happiness.

Similarly, cultivating contentment requires finding fulfillment in the current moment and letting go of the incessant want for more. This doesn't imply settling for mediocrity or complacency but rather learning to accept and enjoy what we have while striving towards our objectives. Mindfulness practices like as meditation and deep breathing can help us create contentment by bringing our focus to the present moment and fostering a sense of inner calm.

In conclusion, while money may surely contribute to our pleasure, its ultimate power rests not in the amassing of riches but in how we choose to utilize it. By emphasizing experiences over stuff, changing our views of success, and fostering appreciation and contentment, we may uncover the key to permanent pleasure and satisfaction in our lives.

CHAPTER 3
MONEY AND RELATIONSHIPS

Money is not only a tool for transactions; it's a dynamic force that may dramatically affect our interactions with others. Whether it's with our spouses, family members, acquaintances, or coworkers, the way we manage money typically reflects deeper parts of our personalities, values, and objectives. In this chapter, we will investigate the complicated interplay between money and relationships, analyzing how financial factors may either enhance or strain the ties we share with others.

Money as a Source of Tension and Conflict

Money has long been acknowledged as one of the primary sources of conflict in partnerships. Disagreements over spending patterns, financial priorities, and unequal contributions to shared costs may lead to anger, irritation, and even marital conflict. For many couples, money talks may be filled with stress, as they manage differences in upbringing, attitudes toward wealth, and financial objectives.

Communicating Effectively about Finances

Effective communication is key for handling financial concerns within relationships. Honest and honest communication about money may help establish trust, understanding, and shared accountability. Couples should establish a safe environment for addressing financial difficulties, expressing their needs and expectations, and cooperatively seeking solutions that correspond with their beliefs and aspirations. Regular check-ins and financial planning meetings may enhance the link between spouses and build a sense of teamwork in handling funds jointly.

Aligning Financial Goals and Values with Partners

One of the keys to financial harmony in partnerships is aligning objectives and ideals with partners. While individuals may have different priorities when it comes to spending, saving, and investing, finding common ground and setting shared objectives may help generate a feeling of unity and purpose. Couples should take the time to address their long-term financial ambitions, such as homeownership, retirement planning, and supporting children's education, and work together to build a roadmap for reaching these goals.

Navigating Differences in Spending and Saving Habits

Differences in spending and saving habits are typical in partnerships and can lead to conflict if not addressed constructively. Couples may have opposing attitudes to money management, with one partner being more thrifty and the other more willing to engage in discretionary purchases. Finding a balance between financial responsibility and enjoying life's joys takes compromise, flexibility, and a desire to understand and appreciate each other's opinions. By identifying and embracing the strengths and distinctions that each spouse brings to the relationship, couples may negotiate financial issues with greater comfort and harmony.

Building Trust and Partnership in Managing Finances Together

Trust is the basis of any healthy relationship, and this holds in areas of financial as well. Couples must trust each other to be truthful, accountable, and responsible in handling joint finances. Building trust involves a commitment to honesty, integrity, and collaborative decision-making. Couples should create clear expectations and boundaries surrounding financial concerns, have open channels of communication, and routinely examine their financial success together. By creating a feeling of cooperation and mutual respect, couples may create a strong financial foundation that improves their bond and boosts their overall relationship pleasure.

In conclusion, money plays a fundamental influence in influencing the dynamics of our relationships. How we handle financial concerns with our spouses, family members, and friends may either build or strain the ties we share with them. By communicating effectively, aligning financial goals and values, navigating differences with empathy and understanding, and building trust and partnership in managing finances together, we can create healthier, more harmonious relationships that thrive on mutual respect, cooperation, and shared prosperity.

investment, as it not only enriches our knowledge and experience but also expands our prospects for growth and financial success. Whether via formal schooling, online courses, or self-directed learning, obtaining new skills and information may open doors to new job pathways, improved earning potential, and more joy in life.

Skill development is equally crucial in today's quickly changing business. As technology continues to change businesses and employment markets, flexibility and versatility are becoming more desirable characteristics. Investing time and effort into obtaining new abilities, staying current with industry trends, and developing existing talents can boost our competitiveness in the job market and raise our earning potential over time.

Self-care routines are vital for sustaining general well-being and resilience amid financial hardship. These may include physical activities such as exercise and diet, as well as mental and emotional practices such as mindfulness, meditation, and therapy. Taking care of our physical, mental, and emotional health not only increases our capacity to cope with stress and hardship but also promotes our clarity of mind, creativity, and decision-making abilities, therefore placing us for better success in our personal and professional lives.

In conclusion, money and personal growth are strongly related. Financial hardships can serve as chances for self-discovery, resilience, and development. By growing resilience, confronting limiting beliefs, and investing in oneself via education, skill development, and self-care routines, we may overcome financial losses with grace and emerge stronger, wiser, and more powerful than before. Ultimately, the road toward financial success is not just about acquiring riches but also about reaching our full potential, pursuing our passions, and living a life of meaning and joy.

CHAPTER 5
MONEY AND SOCIETY

Money is not only a vehicle for individual wealth creation; it is intricately linked with the fabric of society, creating systems, institutions, and the allocation of resources. In this chapter, we will explore the complicated link between money and society, evaluating its role in perpetuating economic inequality, addressing structural challenges of poverty and wealth imbalance, and using wealth as a catalyst for constructive social change.

The Impact of Economic Inequality on Society:

Economic incquality is a major issue that affects cultures across the world. The gap between the affluent and the poor continues to increase, contributing to social unrest, political instability, and limited prospects for upward mobility. At its foundation, economic inequality represents inequities in income, wealth, and access to resources, perpetuating cycles of poverty and marginalization.

One of the most prominent forms of economic inequality is the concentration of wealth within a small fraction of the population. The wealthiest individuals and businesses exercise tremendous influence over economic and political institutions, establishing policies and agendas that typically favor their interests at the expense of the majority.

Moreover, economic disparity exacerbates social divides and destroys social cohesiveness. It generates anger and distrust between various socioeconomic classes, generating tensions and conflicts within communities. In extreme circumstances, it can lead to social unrest, riots, and even revolutions as underprivileged groups demand greater economic fairness and opportunity.

Addressing Systemic Issues of Poverty and Wealth Disparity:

To successfully reduce economic inequality, it is vital to confront the fundamental factors that sustain poverty and wealth imbalance. This needs a multi-faceted strategy that involves legislative measures, social programs, and collective action.

At the policy level, governments play a vital role in enacting measures to redistribute wealth, such as progressive taxation, social assistance programs, and minimum wage regulations. By levying greater taxes on the affluent and companies, governments may create cash to pay for social services and support initiatives that bring people out of poverty.

Additionally, investing in education, healthcare, and infrastructure is vital for establishing possibilities for economic progress and reducing inequality. Access to quality education, in particular, is a significant factor of social mobility, permitting individuals to gain the skills and information needed to prosper in the contemporary economy.

Furthermore, supporting inclusive economic growth involves tackling structural hurdles that perpetuate inequality, such as discrimination based on race, gender, or socioeconomic position. By fostering diversity, equality, and inclusion in the workplace and society at large, we can build a more fair and just society where everyone has the chance to succeed.

Using Wealth as a Tool for Positive Social Change:

While economic disparity offers important issues, money also has the potential to be a catalyst for constructive social change. Many rich individuals and organizations are using their fortunes to solve important social and environmental challenges, ranging from poverty and education to climate change and healthcare.

Philanthropy plays a critical role in mobilizing resources and expertise to confront complicated societal challenges. Through strategic giving and impact investment, donors may support creative solutions and help underrepresented communities overcome hurdles to prosperity.

Moreover, companies have a responsibility to operate ethically and sustainably, considering the larger impact of their activities on society and the environment. Corporate social responsibility (CSR) efforts, such as fair labor standards, environmental stewardship, and community participation, may provide shared benefits for firms and society alike.

In addition to charity and CSR, impact-driven investment is gaining steam as a valuable tool for aligning financial goals with social and environmental objectives. Socially responsible investment (SRI) and environmental, social, and governance (ESG) criteria enable investors to support firms that emphasize sustainability and ethical business practices, creating good change through the capital markets.

Conclusion:

Money is a tremendous force that influences the structure and dynamics of society, impacting everything from economic policy to social conventions and values. Economic disparity offers deep issues, eroding social cohesiveness and prolonging cycles of poverty and marginalization. However, by tackling structural challenges and harnessing money as a catalyst for positive social change, we can build a more fair and inclusive society where everyone has the chance to prosper. Through collective action, ethical governance, and conscious capitalism, we can harness the power of money to construct a more equitable and sustainable world for future generations.

CHAPTER 6
MONEY AND SPIRITUALITY

Money and spirituality are typically seen as opposing factors, with money symbolizing materialism and spirituality signifying transcendence. However, a closer investigation reveals that these two domains are inextricably connected, and comprehending their relationship may lead to great personal growth and joy.

Exploring the Spiritual Dimensions of Money:

Money is more than just a vehicle of commerce; it bears symbolic and energetic meaning. In many spiritual traditions, money is considered a mirror of one's values, beliefs, and intentions. How we earn, spend, and manage money reflects our connection with ourselves, others, and the world around us.

One of the essential spiritual components of money is the notion of abundance awareness against scarcity thinking. Abundance awareness is the conviction that there are more than enough resources to go around and that we are innately deserving of wealth. On the other side, a scarcity mindset is founded on fear and lack, leading to hoarding, competitiveness, and feelings of inadequacy.

Overcoming the Myth of Scarcity:

Many people operate from a mindset of scarcity, believing that there is not enough money or chances to go around. This thinking can lead to emotions of worry, avarice, and unhappiness. However, by growing abundant consciousness, we may adjust our viewpoint and perceive the richness that already exists in our lives.

Practices such as gratitude, visualization, and affirmations can help reprogram our minds to concentrate on plenty rather than lack. By identifying and appreciating the benefits in our lives, we draw greater abundance into our experience. Visualizing our objectives and wants as already realized helps match our thoughts and actions with our intentions, generating a positive feedback cycle of abundance.

Aligning Financial Goals with Spiritual Values:

Spirituality invites us to examine our beliefs and objectives and link them with our financial goals. What do we genuinely appreciate in life? What provides us joy and fulfillment? By identifying our values and adopting goals that are in harmony with them, we may generate a feeling of purpose and meaning in our financial efforts.

For example, if we value connection and community, we may prioritize spending money on experiences with loved ones rather than tangible items. If we value personal growth and contribution, we may invest in education, self-development, and charity activities that match our values.

Practices for Cultivating Mindfulness and Presence:

Mindfulness is the discipline of being completely present and aware of our thoughts, feelings, and experiences in the present moment. When it comes to money, mindfulness may help us make thoughtful and empowered financial decisions rather than responding on autopilot or impulse.

Mindful spending requires pausing and contemplating before making a purchase, asking ourselves if it corresponds with our beliefs and goals. Mindful earning entails finding employment that is meaningful and gratifying, where our abilities and interests fit with our purpose. Mindful giving includes sharing our resources with others in a way that is generous and compassionate.

Finding Meaning and Purpose Beyond Material Wealth:

Ultimately, genuine wealth is not defined by the size of our bank accounts but by the richness of our lives. Spirituality urges us to discover meaning and purpose beyond worldly goods and external successes. It urges us to nurture values such as love, compassion, and inner serenity, which are genuine sources of satisfaction and pleasure.

Money may be a great instrument for promoting our spiritual growth and achieving our mission in the world. When utilized with awareness and intention, money may be a vehicle for producing good change and making a difference in the lives of others. By matching our financial objectives with our spiritual beliefs and cultivating abundant consciousness, we may unleash the true potential of money to build a life of purpose, fulfillment, and abundance.

CONCLUSION

In our investigation of the power of money, we've walked through its numerous facets, finding its psychological, social, and philosophical ramifications. From comprehending the delicate link between money and happiness to diving into its influence on relationships, personal growth, society, and spirituality, we've learned vital insights into the transforming potential of money in our lives.

First and foremost, we've understood that money is not only a method of commerce or a measure of wealth; it is a symbol of value and worth firmly imprinted in our brains. Our views towards money are affected by a complex interaction of circumstances, including childhood experiences, societal conventions, and personal convictions. By noticing and understanding these effects, we may begin to create a healthier and more powerful relationship with money.

One of the important surprises on our path has been the knowledge that genuine pleasure does not come from the amassing of material stuff but from the richness of experiences and connections. While money might bring comfort and security, its power to buy happiness is limited. Instead, we've realized that fostering thankfulness, happiness, and meaningful connections with people are vital elements for a full existence.

In examining the complexities of money and relationships, we've seen the obstacles and opportunities that come when dollars interact with love and collaboration. Effective communication, alignment of values, and mutual respect are vital for negotiating the intricacies of financial concerns within partnerships. By cultivating openness, trust, and cooperation, we may change money from a source of conflict into a vehicle for establishing better ties and shared dreams.

Our investigation has also shed light on the important relationship between money and human growth. Financial success is not only about acquiring riches; it is about the path of self-discovery, resilience, and empowerment. By reframing financial challenges as opportunities for growth, embracing risk-taking, and investing in ourselves, we can unleash our full potential and build the life we love.

Furthermore, we've gone into the sociopolitical ramifications of money, facing questions of economic injustice, privilege, and social justice. While money may be a source of empowerment for some, it is a barrier for others. Addressing systemic imbalances and pushing for good social change are crucial steps toward achieving a more just and equitable society where everyone has the opportunity to prosper.

Finally, we've investigated the spiritual elements of money, overcoming its materialistic implications to reveal its greater importance. By adopting abundant consciousness, connecting our financial objectives with our spiritual beliefs, and exercising mindfulness in our financial decision-making, we may experience a profound feeling of purpose, meaning, and fulfillment in our lives.

In summary, the power of money is both enormous and profound. It can mold our destinies, affect our choices, and affect our relationships with ourselves, others, and the world around us. By harnessing its power with intention, integrity, and compassion, we may build a life of abundance, fulfillment, and meaning. Let us go on this journey with open hearts and minds, embracing the transforming power of money to enhance not just our own lives but the lives of others as well.

www.ingramcontent.com/pod-product-compliance
Lightning Source LLC
Chambersburg PA
CBHW070957220526
45471CB00007B/3075